WACO-McLENNAN
1717 AUS
WACO TX

JUSTICE, POLICING, AND THE RULE OF LAW

FOUNDATIONS OF DEMOCRACY

FOUNDATIONS OF DEMOCRACY

JUSTICE, POLICING, AND THE RULE OF LAW

Author and Series Advisor

Tom Lansford
Professor of Political Science
University of Southern Mississippi, Gulf Coast

MASON CREST

Mason Crest
450 Parkway Drive, Suite D
Broomall, PA 19008
www.masoncrest.com

MTM Publishing, Inc.
435 West 23rd Street, #8C
New York, NY 10011
www.mtmpublishing.com

President: Valerie Tomaselli
Vice President, Book Development: Hilary Poole
Designer: Annemarie Redmond
Copyeditor: Peter Jaskowiak
Editorial Assistant: Andrea St. Aubin

Series ISBN: 978-1-4222-3625-3
Hardback ISBN: 978-1-4222-3630-7
E-Book ISBN: 978-1-4222-8274-8

Library of Congress Cataloging-in-Publication Data
Names: Lansford, Tom, author.
Title: Justice, policing, and the rule of law / by Tom Lansford.
Description: Broomall, PA: Mason Crest, 2017. | Series: Foundations of
  democracy | Includes index.
Identifiers: LCCN 2016004311 | ISBN 9781422236307 (hardback) | ISBN
  9781422282748 (ebook)
Subjects: LCSH: Justice, Administration of—Juvenile literature. | Law
  enforcement—Juvenile literature.
Classification: LCC K2100 .L36 2017 | DDC 364—dc23
LC record available at http://lccn.loc.gov/2016004311

Printed and bound in the United States of America.

First printing
9 8 7 6 5 4 3 2 1

TABLE OF CONTENTS

Key Icons to Look for:

Words to Understand: These words with their easy-to-understand definitions will increase the reader's understanding of the text, while building vocabulary skills.

Sidebars: This boxed material within the main text allows readers to build knowledge, gain insights, explore possibilities, and broaden their perspectives by weaving together additional information to provide realistic and holistic perspectives.

Research Projects: Readers are pointed toward areas of further inquiry connected to each chapter. Suggestions are provided for projects that encourage deeper research and analysis.

Text-Dependent Questions: These questions send the reader back to the text for more careful attention to the evidence presented there.

Series Glossary of Key Terms: This back-of-the-book glossary contains terminology used throughout the series. Words found here increase the reader's ability to read and comprehend higher-level books and articles in this field.

Iraqi women at a political rally in 2010, in advance of the country's parliamentary elections.

SERIES INTRODUCTION

Democracy is a form of government in which the people hold all or most of the political power. In democracies, government officials are expected to take actions and implement policies that reflect the will of the majority of the citizenry. In other political systems, the rulers generally rule for their own benefit, or at least they usually put their own interests first. This results in deep differences between the rulers and the average citizen. In undemocratic states, elites enjoy far more privileges and advantages than the average citizen. Indeed, autocratic governments are often created to exploit the average citizen.

Elections allow citizens to choose representatives to make choices for them, and under some circumstances to decide major issues themselves. Yet democracy is much more than campaigns and elections. Many nations conduct elections but are not democratic. True democracy is dependent on a range of freedoms for its citizenry, and it simultaneously exists to protect and enhance those freedoms. At its best, democracy ensures that elites, average citizens, and even groups on the margins of society all have the same rights, privileges, and opportunities. The components of democracy have changed over time as individuals and groups have struggled to expand equality. In doing so, the very notion of what makes up a democracy has evolved. The volumes in this series examine the core freedoms that form the foundation of modern democracy.

Citizenship and Immigration explores what it means to be a citizen in a democracy. The principles of democracy are based on equality, liberty, and government by the consent of the people. Equality means that all citizens have the same rights and responsibilities. Democracies have struggled to integrate all groups and ensure full equality. Citizenship in a democracy is the formal recognition that a person is a member of the country's political community. Modern democracies have faced profound debates over immigration, especially how many people to admit to the country and what rights to confer on immigrants who are not citizens.

Challenges have also emerged within democracies over how to ensure disadvantaged groups enjoy full equality with the majority, or traditionally dominant, populations. While outdated legal or political barriers have been mostly removed, democracies still struggle to overcome cultural or economic impediments to equality. *Gender Equality and Identity Rights* analyzes why gender equality has proven especially challenging, requiring political, economic, and cultural reforms. Concurrently, *Religious, Cultural, and Minority Rights* surveys the efforts that democracies have undertaken to integrate disadvantaged groups into the political, economic, and social mainstream.

A free and unfettered media provides an important check on government power and ensures an informed citizenry. The importance of free expression and a free press are detailed in *Speech, Media, and Protest*, while *Employment and Workers' Rights* provides readers with an overview of the importance of economic liberty and the ways in which employment and workers' rights reinforce equality by guaranteeing opportunity.

The maintenance of both liberty and equality requires a legal system in which the police are constrained by the rule of law. This means that security officials understand and respect the rights of individuals and groups and use their power in a manner that benefits communities, not represses them. While this is the ideal, legal systems continue to struggle to achieve equality, especially among disadvantaged groups. These topics form the core of *Justice, Policing, and the Rule of Law*.

Corruption and Transparency examines the greatest danger to democracy: corruption. Corruption can undermine people's faith in government and erode equality. Transparency, or open government, provides the best means to prevent corruption by ensuring that the decisions and actions of officials are easily understood.

As discussed in *Political Participation and Voting Rights*, a government of the people requires its citizens to provide regular input on policies and decisions through consultations and voting. Despite the importance of voting, the history of democracies has been marked by the struggle to expand voting rights. Many groups, including women, only gained the right to vote in the last century, and continue to be underrepresented in political office.

Ultimately, all of the foundations of democracy are interrelated. Equality ensures liberty, while liberty helps maintain equality. Meanwhile, both are necessary for a government by consent to be effective and lasting. Within a democracy, all people must be treated equally and be able to enjoy the full range of liberties of the country, including rights such as free speech, religion, and voting.

—Tom Lansford

CHAPTER ONE

JUSTICE

WORDS TO UNDERSTAND

community service: unpaid work, usually done to benefit the community; can be imposed as a penalty for wrongdoing.

justice: the process by which a country's legal system ensures that people are treated fairly and obey laws.

property crimes: crimes that consist of taking, or destroying, property, usually without the use of force or intimidation.

restorative justice: a criminal justice system that concentrates on reconciliation and rehabilitation between criminals and their community.

retributive justice: a legal approach that emphasizes proportionate punishment for criminals instead of rehabilitation.

At its most basic level, **justice** is simply ensuring that everyone gets what they deserve. People who behave and follow the rules of a society should be rewarded, while people who misbehave or commit crimes should be punished. From this perspective, justice is synonymous with fairness. It is also tied to the notion of equality, that all people should be treated the same.

The reverse side of Paraguay's flag displays the nation's motto, "Peace and Justice."

Justice is the one of the fundamental elements of democracy. For democracy to be effective, governments must promote justice and equality. If citizens believe that a country's laws, institutions, and public officials are fair and just, they are more likely to trust the government. People are also more likely to obey laws and support their leaders. The importance of justice is often highlighted in the constitutions and founding documents of nations. It also appears in national mottos and the pledges of countries. For instance, the motto of Paraguay is "Peace and Justice," while the U.S. Pledge of Allegiance ends with the phrase "liberty and justice for all."

The idea of justice is at the heart of any nation's legal system. The laws, courts, and the police, which make up a legal system, all have a role to play in promoting justice. People expect that if someone commits a crime, the legal or justice system will impose the appropriate punishment. Yet people also expect that victims of crime should be compensated. Laws need to be just and be administered justly, or people will lose faith in the legal system.

RETRIBUTIVE JUSTICE

When most people think of justice, they are envisioning **retributive justice**. Retributive justice is based on the principle that those who commit wrongdoing must be punished for their misdeeds. It is the most common approach used by legal systems, and it has a long history. One of the earliest recorded legal codes, the Code of Hammurabi, from approximately 1754 BCE, describes a variety of punishments for various crimes, including the famous requirement that "if a man destroy the eye of another man, they shall destroy his eye"; this is frequently shortened to the concept of "an eye for an eye."

For retributive justice to be effective, punishments must be proportionate to crimes, hence the common phrase "the punishment must fit the crime." If penalties are

THE CODE OF HAMMURABI

King Hammurabi ruled the Babylonian Empire from approximately 1792 to 1750 BCE. During his reign a series of laws were codified into what became known as the Code of Hammurabi. The Code included 282 laws that defined what punishments would be awarded for specific crimes. For instance, the code states, "If any one commits a robbery and is caught, then he shall be put to death." The code also includes stipulations on how much could be charged by professionals such as physicians. In his introduction to the laws, Hammurabi declared that he developed the Code "to bring about the rule of righteousness in the land, to destroy the wicked and the evil-doers; so that the strong should not harm the weak." The Code was discovered by archaeologists in 1901 in Iran.

The Code of Hammurabi, on display at the Louvre Museum in Paris.

disproportionate to transgressions, people lose faith in the justice system. For instance, in Great Britain in the 1700s, hanging was the punishment for more than 200 crimes, many of which would be considered relatively minor today, like picking pockets or breaking into a house. In modern democracies, justice systems impose a variety of punishments, from minor to severe. Small crimes such as speeding or loitering typically have fines of between $25 to $100. More serious offenses result in confinement in prison or even capital punishment (execution) in some countries.

Retributive justice is designed to accomplish three main goals. The first is to deter wrongdoing. If people believe they might be apprehended and punished for a crime, they may be less likely to commit the offense. The second goal is to provide a sense of justice, to make people feel that the government is protecting them or their property by punishing criminals. The third and final goal is the removal of criminals from society. Someone who commits a serious crime and is sent to prison for a lengthy period is unable to engage in further misdeeds against the public while incarcerated.

RESTORATIVE JUSTICE

Although retributive justice is common, it is not the only way to approach the issue. Restorative justice concentrates on two problems. The first is the rehabilitation of those who have committed criminal offenses. The second is the repair of any harm done by criminal acts through redress for the victims of criminal offenses. To accomplish these two very different goals, restorative justice takes a collective approach that involves interaction by the wrongdoer, the victims of a crime, representatives of the community, and law enforcement. All of the involved parties work together to craft a solution that repairs the harm done to the victim and the community by the crime, while giving the perpetrator the opportunity to make amends.

In countries or communities that use restorative justice, the victim and representatives of the community, usually government officials, negotiate a process, whereby the offender accepts responsibility for his or her wrongdoing and provides

COMMUNITY SERVICE

Community service is a common sentence in both retributive justice and restorative justice. In retributive justice, community service is often used as a punishment for minor crimes, as a way to reduce crowding in prisons and to serve as a deterrent (you will often see offenders working in public). In restorative justice, the sentence is seen as a way for the offender to give back to the community. Common forms of community service include cleaning public areas, such as parks or highways, and performing minor maintenance such as painting buildings or cutting grass. Community service may also include speaking to groups at risk for committing crimes, including juveniles.

A community service work detail for the 35th District Court, in Northville, Michigan.

The courthouse in Balmain, a suburb of Sydney, Australia.

some form of restitution. This may be in the form of financial payments, the return or replacement of stolen or damaged property, or even **community service**. Offenders may also be required to attend counseling. Restorative justice does not mean that an offender never serves a prison sentence, but it provides a way for the criminal to be rehabilitated into the community. Restorative justice is usually not utilized for severe crimes such as murder.

Restorative justice is a relatively new approach to crime, but it is increasingly being used by many democracies around the world. For instance, in Austria, since 2000, restorative justice has been used for minor crimes such as theft. The result is that fewer people go to jail, while victims report more satisfaction with the legal system and a sense that they have recovered from any losses or damages. Other countries that have instituted restorative justice programs—especially with regard to juvenile justice— include Australia, Brazil, Canada, and Great Britain.

Distributive Justice

Distributive justice is the effort by public institutions to ensure that everyone has access to what they need in life. Also known as social justice, this approach focuses mainly on economic and social equality. The goal is not for everyone to have the same wealth or property, but for everyone's basic needs to be met in a healthy society.

Communities with high crime rates often also have other problems, such as high unemployment, substandard housing, and inadequate education. This reflects a broader link between poverty and certain types of crime. Studies in Ireland found that 60 percent of those convicted of minor crimes, such as theft, lived in poverty, and more than 70 percent of those in prison were unemployed before they committed the crimes for which they were incarcerated. The poor are also more likely to be victims of crime than the affluent.

The obvious conclusion is that one way to reduce crime is to reduce poverty. Governments that are better able to promote economic and social equality are also

CAPITAL PUNISHMENT

Capital punishment, also known as the death penalty, has fallen out of favor among democratic countries. Democracies from Australia to Canada to South Africa, and including all of the nations of Western Europe, have abolished capital punishment. According to Amnesty International, 101 countries had eliminated the death penalty by July 2015. Twenty-two nations, including the United States, China, India, and Japan, continue to use capital punishment. In the United States, 31 states use the death penalty, while 19 and the District of Columbia do not. Texas executes more prisoners than any other state, with 531 executions between 1982 and November 2015.

Countries that utilize the death penalty contend the punishment deters criminals and provides the ultimate justice for those that commit crimes such as murder. Opponents of capital punishment point out that mistakes have been made whereby some people who were innocent were executed. They also contend that the death penalty is immoral and that nations should not execute their own citizens.

COUNTRIES WITH THE HIGHEST NUMBER OF EXECUTIONS, 2013*

Country	Number of executions
Iran	369
Iraq	169
Saudi Arabia	79
North Korea	70
United States	39

*China is estimated to execute more than 1,000 people per year, but does not provide official statistics on its use of the death penalty.

Source: Leila Haddou, "Death Penalty Statistics 2013: County by Country," *The Guardian*, March 27, 2014. http://www.theguardian.com/world/datablog/2014/mar/27/death-penalty-statistics-2013-by-country.

better able to lower crime rates. With lower poverty rates, people are less likely to commit **property crimes**, because they have greater access to consumer goods and more to lose if they are caught engaging in wrongdoing. For instance, someone convicted of a serious crime often loses his or her job. Better education, worker training, and improvements in housing are all steps that governments may undertake to reduce poverty. Consequently, economic equality emerges as an important form of justice.

TEXT-DEPENDENT QUESTIONS

1. What are the three main goals of retributive justice?
2. What problems are addressed by restorative justice?
3. How does poverty affect crime rates?

RESEARCH PROJECTS

1. Study retributive justice and restorative justice. Create a chart that compares and contrasts the two approaches to criminal justice.
2. Research capital punishment. Write a brief report on the arguments for and against the death penalty, and create a chart that contrasts those arguments.

CHAPTER TWO

THE JUSTICE SYSTEM

WORDS TO UNDERSTAND

civil law: statutes and rules that govern private rights and responsibilities and regulate noncriminal disputes over issues such as property or contracts.

criminal law: statutes and rules that govern punishment for offenses prohibited by the government.

defendant: the person, group, organization, or business that is accused of wrongdoing in court.

ombudsman: an official who is appointed to investigate complaints against a government agency or other institution.

plaintiff: someone who files a complaint against someone else in court. Private individuals, groups, organizations, or businesses are usually the plaintiffs in civil cases, while the government is typically the plaintiff, or represents the plaintiff, in criminal matters.

precedents: a legal decision that guides or influences subsequent court cases.

probation: a legal sentence that allows a convict to be released from prison, under supervision, for a specified period of time, subject to good behavior.

A mosaic portrait of Emperor Justinian I, from the Basilica of San Vitale, in Rome.

I n order to promote justice, states rely on an elaborate network of agencies and institutions known as the *justice system* or *legal system*. In many cases, these systems have evolved over hundreds of years. The two most commonly used legal systems among democracies are *common law* and *Roman law*. Common law is a legal system based on English law and that evolved from customs and judicial **precedents**. Some early precedents in English common law date back to the 1100s. Countries with connections to Great Britain, including former colonies, have legal systems based on common law, including Australia, Canada, the United States, and South Africa. Roman law has its roots in the laws codes of the East Roman (Byzantine) emperor Justinian from about 600 CE. It is based on existing statues as opposed to precedents. Most Continental European countries, as well as the states of Latin America and Japan, use Roman law. There are about 150 countries that utilize Roman law, while around 80 use common law.

The two traditions take different approaches to justice. In Roman law traditions, judges play a key role in the court proceedings and are charged with discovering the truth. Judges often question witnesses and have investigatory responsibilities. In contrast, in common law countries, judges act as neutral referees between the **plaintiff** and the **defendant**. Lawyers typically question the plaintiff, defendant, and any witnesses.

In Roman law countries, justices have little discretion in their rulings and are charged with following the letter of the law. In common law countries, judges often have wide latitude in

An English barrister (a type of lawyer) enters the Chelmsford Crown Court in 2015.

Family law is a huge part of the civil justice system.

sentencing, and their decisions are usually binding on other, similar cases. (One major exception to this in the United States is drug law, in which sentencing requirements are written into the law, rather than decided by judges.) In general, common law systems tend to have a greater emphasis on the *process* of the legal system; violations of process may result in the removal of charges against defendants.

While there can be significant differences between the justice systems of various countries, there are some key similarities. All true justice systems are built upon the foundation of equality. Everyone must be treated the same, whether they are old or young, rich or poor, or famous or infamous. This means that laws and procedures have to be created and implemented in such a way that one group is not given preferential treatment. It also requires officials in the criminal justice system to be fair and impartial. Impartiality is critically important to justice systems because it is necessary to secure the trust of people.

Transparency is also an essential element of a justice system. People must be able to witness and understand why decisions are made and why they are implemented in certain ways. In order to ensure transparency, legal proceedings are usually open to the public in democratic nations, though sometimes there are exceptions to protect the identity of witnesses or sensitive information. The results of such proceedings are also public. Despite differences in history or tradition, equality and transparency are the hallmarks of legal systems in democratic nations.

JUSTICE SYSTEMS

Justice systems in democracies are typically divided into two broad categories: **civil law** and **criminal law**. Both categories include a wide range of professionals, including lawyers who represent the interests of participants in the process. Civil justice systems focus on noncriminal matters. They offer people an opportunity to pursue justice for wrongs that are not illegal, but that do cause some type of harm. They also provide a means to settle disputes between plaintiffs and defendants.

Family law is one of the largest areas of civil justice and includes issues such as marriage and divorce, child custody, adoption, and inheritance. It is also one of the most contentious areas of law, since it involves children and family relations. Countries often have special courts to deal with family law. In Australia, for instance, the highest legal body on family law is appropriately named the Family Court.

Civil justice also covers areas such as property and contract disputes. Some of these disagreements involve large corporations and significant sums of money. For instance, in 2010 a court ruled that the company AT&T owed California telephone users more than $16.5 million for overcharging consumers in violation of their contracts.

Torts are actions that cause economic, physical, or emotional harm to someone else and require some type of compensation. Examples of torts include automobile accidents, personal injuries, and damage to property. Different countries deal with torts in different fashions. For instance, in New Zealand, when people suffer a medical injury, the

TORTS

There are two main classifications of torts. The first is intentional torts. These occur when the plaintiff deliberately sets out to do harm to the defendant. An example of an intentional tort would be assault, an effort to physically harm someone or create an atmosphere of fear. If a person displayed a baseball bat in a threatening manner, that would be assault, even if there was no physical contact (if there is contact, then it becomes assault and battery).

The second type is negligence torts, which occur when harm is done without intent. Negligence torts require that the plaintiff prove that the defendant *should* have recognized that his or her action could cause harm but failed to take appropriate steps to prevent that harm.

Car accidents are much more likely to be negligence torts, rather than intentional torts.

government compensates them, instead of allowing them to sue the doctor or hospital. In the United States, a plaintiff might take the doctor or hospital to court to recover not only direct losses, but also to be compensated for any additional pain or mental suffering from their actions.

Criminal Justice Systems

Criminal justice systems determine guilt or innocence in criminal matters and allocate and oversee punishment for wrongdoing. Criminal justice has three main components: law enforcement, criminal courts, and the corrections system.

French police officers in Nice during a student protest in 2010.

PUBLIC DEFENDERS

In just societies, those accused of crimes have a right to defend themselves. In democracies, defendants have a number of legal protections. In most democracies, defendants have the right to an attorney to help in their defense. If they cannot afford a lawyer, the government will provide one (known as a public defender). For instance, the Brazilian Constitution established a public defenders' office to provide professional lawyers for the poor. In other countries, such as the United Kingdom, private lawyers work with poor defendants, but are paid by the government. However, some democracies do not provide public defenders in all cases. For instance, Singapore only provides public defenders in criminal cases that involve the death penalty.

Law enforcement officials are in charge of investigating crimes, gathering evidence, and questioning and (if appropriate) arresting suspects (see chapter three). Law enforcement plays a major role in deterring crime. Sometimes that deterrence is simply by their presence. At other times, investigators are able to gain foreknowledge of a crime and arrest the potential wrongdoers for conspiracy. Law enforcement is the largest component of the criminal justice system. For instance, in France, there are more than 220,000 police officers for a population of about 64 million, but only about 65,000 judges, prosecutors, and various court clerks and other staff.

The second area of the criminal justice system is the courts. Criminal courts hear cases that involve activities that the government has declared illegal. Defendants may be tried before a judge, a panel of judges, or a jury. Most nations only use jury trials in criminal cases (the United States and Canada are among the few nations that use juries in civil trials). Courts determine the guilt or innocence of defendants, and then decide punishment. To ensure justice, legal proceedings are typically organized to ensure that the defendant has the opportunity to defend himself or herself in court.

Office of the Ombudsman for the Czech Republic

The corrections system includes prisons and other detention facilities, as well as programs to monitor sentences that do not involve incarceration, such as community service or **probation**. The increased use of restorative justice has reduced the number of people in prison in countries such as Australia, Belgium, and New Zealand.

Nontraditional Approaches to Justice

As part of a broad effort to reduce the number of court cases and the costs associated with torts, many countries have adopted a process called *alternative dispute resolution* (ADR). ADR is a means of settling a dispute without involving traditional courts. A common form of ADR is *arbitration*, in which both sides in a dispute agree to accept the decision of a neutral party, often a retired judge or other legal professional (sometimes an arbitration panel with multiple members is utilized). The arbitrator hears both sides of the dispute, reviews the evidence, and then issues a decision. Arbitration is much faster and usually less expensive than going to court. In India, the government encourages businesses to have arbitration agreements as part of their contracts with each other.

A second form of ADR is *mediation*, in which the parties in a disagreement agree to have an outsider or external group attempt to craft a mutually agreed-upon solution to their dispute. Unlike arbitration, the parties in mediation do not have to accept the recommendations of the mediator. This process increases the pressure to find a compromise that is acceptable to all involved. Sometimes parties are more willing to enter into mediation than arbitration since they know they will not be bound by the findings of a mediator.

Governments increasingly use **ombudsmen** to investigate complaints by citizens against public agencies or government officials, including law enforcement. An ombudsman may also use arbitration or mediation to settle disputes, or may recommendation action against officials within an agency. Sweden makes extensive use of ombudsmen and has separate ombudsman departments for areas such as children's welfare, consumer issues, and citizen's equality.

TEXT-DEPENDENT QUESTIONS

1. Which countries are most likely to use common law?
2. What are the three main areas of the criminal justice system?
3. What are the most common forms of alternative dispute resolution?

RESEARCH PROJECTS

1. Research common law and Roman law systems. Decide which system you believe is superior to the other, and write an essay defending that choice.
2. Research alternative dispute resolution (ADR). Write a report that explains how ADR can reduce legal costs.

CHAPTER THREE

POLICING

WORDS TO UNDERSTAND

cybercrime: illicit activity involving computers or the Internet; examples include hacking into someone else's electronic devices to obtain personal information or the spread of malicious software such as viruses.

DNA: deoxyribonucleic acid, or DNA, contains the genetic codes of living beings, including plants and animals; it can be used as a tool to identify an individual in criminal cases.

identity theft: the appropriation of someone's personal information for criminal activity, such as obtaining false credit or improperly purchasing items.

jurisdiction: the official authority to administer justice through activities such as investigations, arrests, and obtaining testimony.

taser: a device that fires electronic barbs, or delivers an electronic shock, that is capable of causing temporary paralysis.

P olicing, or law enforcement, involves a wide variety of activities that government bodies undertake to keep the peace and maintain public order. As noted above, it is the largest element of the criminal justice system. It is also an area that raises significant concerns about justice. On the one hand, the basic function of policing is to ensure justice. On the other hand, law enforcement officials often use tactics and techniques that would be unjust under other circumstances. For instance, police have the power to detain suspects against their will and to use deadly force.

Ancient societies organized their police forces in a variety of ways. In Asian societies, such as China, Japan, and Korea, officials known as prefects were given responsibility for law enforcement. In other cultures, including the Roman Empire, the military played a large role in policing by providing security and apprehending criminals. In Europe during the Middle Ages, localities often hired watchmen to patrol cities and prevent crimes. In England, these watchmen were members of the community and were usually under the supervision of someone appointed as a constable. In rural areas, a *shire reeve*, or sheriff, was appointed by the monarch to keep the peace.

The professional police force established in London in 1829 became a model for other countries. The policemen were nicknamed "bobbies" or "peelers" after Sir Robert Peel, who pushed for the creation of the force (British police officers are still called bobbies). The members of the force were trained and wore uniforms, and had wide **jurisdiction** within the community.

PRINCIPLES OF POLICING

Modern policing is based on three main principles. The first is prevention. Law enforcement officers seek to prevent wrongdoing through a variety of techniques. For example, the police work with members of the community to make their homes or businesses more secure by pointing out ways that thieves might access their property. They could further make suggestions on crime-prevention measures such as better locks, video monitoring, or the use of safes. Police also provide information on crimes or criminals in an area so that citizens know if they need to be extra vigilant. Law enforcement could also support neighborhood watches or provide education about crime through public forums or programs on issues such as **cybercrime** or **identity theft**.

A portrait of Robert Peel, who is considered to be the creator of the first modern police force, in London in the 19th century.

The second principle is deterrence. While crime prevention relies on community participation, deterrence emphasizes the role of law enforcement. Just the presence of police officers can prevent crime, which is why regular patrols through neighborhoods are highly important. Police officers also need to develop good intelligence networks that can alert them to potential crimes. Law enforcement officials have also found that strict enforcement of traffic laws or other measures that bring them into regular contact with the public, often allows officers to learn about, or deter, crime. For instance, a traffic stop might result in preventing a future robbery or assault by allowing an officer to search a vehicle or person.

The third principle is investigation. If a crime has been committed, police must swiftly and efficiently investigate the wrongdoing and apprehend the offender. Investigations typically combine personal interaction with the increased use of technology. For instance, police must interview witnesses and seek clues at a crime

THE 1829 PRINCIPLES OF POLICING

When Sir Robert Peel (1788–1850) attempted to establish the first modern police force, he faced widespread opposition. Many people feared that the police force would be used by the government to repress dissent or criticism of officials. To dispel these fears, the new police adopted nine principles to secure public trust. The values all emphasized the need to maintain the confidence of the public and several stressed the need to only use force when all other alternatives had been tried. For instance, Principle 2 declared that the "power of the police to fulfil their functions and duties is dependent on public approval of their existence, actions and behavior, and on their ability to secure and maintain public respect." Principle 3 stated that officers should "recognize always that the extent to which the cooperation of the public can be secured diminishes proportionately the necessity of the use of physical force and compulsion for achieving police objectives." To emphasize that force was a last resort, the London Metropolitan Police did not carry firearms.

Source: UK Home Office, "Definition of Policing by Consent," December 10, 2012. https://www.gov.uk/government/publications/policing-by-consent.

Signpost for a neighborhood crime watch in Elko, Nevada.

scene. Interviewing witnesses and suspects is commonly known as interrogating and is a specialized skill among many law enforcement officers. Technology also helps police investigations. For instance, police use fingerprint evidence to help prove an offender was at a crime (all humans have distinct fingerprints). **DNA** evidence can also help establish the guilt or innocence of a suspect. Other useful forms of technology range from video-camera recordings to phone or electronic records and tests that determine if someone has fired a gun.

POLICE AND THE USE OF FORCE

One of the most controversial features of policing is the use of force. Police around the world are authorized to use force to detain suspects and prevent or stop crimes. However, before resorting to force, law enforcement officers are trained to use techniques such as persuasion, warnings, and even the threat of violence to convince people to comply with commands or stop illicit behavior. In democratic countries it is generally understood that physical force should only be used as a last resort when there are no other options, and when the officer's life, or the lives of nearby civilians, is in danger.

When using force, police officers utilize a range of possibilities. Batons and clubs are commonly issued to police, as are chemical agents such as pepper spray or tear gas and electronic devices such as **tasers**. These weapons may injure a suspect, but are usually, though not always, nonlethal. Police may also use nonlethal bullets (often rubber bullets) or even water cannons to disperse crowds. Sometimes, law enforcement even uses animals, such as dogs and horses, to control people's actions.

When there is no other option, police may have to resort to the use of deadly force with a weapon such as a handgun, shotgun, or rifle. In some countries, guns are standard issue to members of the police. In other nations, the police normally do not carry weapons; these include Iceland, Ireland, New Zealand, Norway, and the United Kingdom. Instead, there are special police units that are trained to use weapons and are deployed when needed during crimes such as armed robbery or other acts of violence.

A SWAT team on alert. The term SWAT stands for Special Weapons and Tactics.

Even forces that carry sidearms also have heavily armed and trained units. For instance, in the United States, these are known as Special Weapons and Tactics (SWAT) teams, while in France they are known as the Intervention Groups of the National Police. The use of deadly force is explored in more detail in the final chapter.

POLICE AROUND THE WORLD

Countries organize their law enforcement agencies in different ways. Many nations divide their police forces between national and local law enforcement. National police forces usually have the same powers as local agencies, but they are able to exercise that authority anywhere in the nation, whereas local police have limited areas of authority. For example, in France, cities may have local police forces with narrow jurisdictions that are responsible to an area's mayor. They also have limited powers to investigate crimes. The national police have power throughout the country, perform most major investigations, and report to the minister of the interior of the central government. The French also have a third law enforcement branch known as the *gendarme*. This force is part of the military and responds

POLICE ANIMALS

Many police forces use animals for various duties. For instance, because of their heightened sense of smell, dogs may be utilized to track suspects or identify hidden items including illicit drugs or explosive material. Search-and-rescue dogs are trained to find missing people or recover cadavers. Dogs are also used by police forces to subdue suspects or intimidate people. Breeds such as bloodhounds or beagles are commonly used as detection animals, while larger breeds such as German shepherds, rottweilers, and Labrador retrievers are often used for other purposes.

Other animals commonly used include horses, which are often used to patrol or control crowds. Sometimes police use exotic animals for specialized purposes. For instance, police forces in Japan have used docile cats to help calm people during interviews.

A German shepherd police dog in training.

to major crimes such as terrorist attacks, riots, or other forms of civil unrest. It also provides law enforcement in rural areas without local police forces.

The police forces of democratic nations have several principles in common. The first is civilian oversight. In a democracy, elected officials or members of the community hold ultimate responsibility for the police, including the ability to make decisions on funding and conduct. Civilian oversight may also be expressed through the election of law enforcement officials, such as elected sheriffs. Second, the police must also be subject to the law; that is, police officers should be both bound by the law *and* authorized to enforce it. Police officers who violate the law are, in theory, subject to the same criminal justice procedures as other suspects. Third, there must be robust protections for people accused of crimes or illicit behavior. This protects the innocent and ensures people have faith in their nation's policing system.

TEXT-DEPENDENT QUESTIONS

1. What are the principles of policing?
2. What types of nonlethal force are commonly used by police officers?
3. Name three things that are common to police forces in democratic countries?

RESEARCH PROJECTS

1. Research the election of law enforcement officials. Is it a good or bad idea to elect police officials? Write a brief report that discusses the positive and negative aspects of such elections.
2. Study the question of whether police officers should carry guns. Compare two countries, one where law enforcement officers carry sidearms and one where officers do not, and highlight the differences in how those nations deal with violent suspects.

CHAPTER FOUR

THE RULE OF LAW

WORDS TO UNDERSTAND

appeal: to request that a higher court review the ruling of a lower one.

checks and balances: a separation of powers among different agencies or branches of government that is designed to ensure that no single individual, group, or component dominates the political process by accruing too much authority.

chief executive: the principle leader of a government, business, or organization.

due process: the guarantee that people cannot be deprived of life, liberty, or property, without fair and just legal proceedings.

human rights: rights that everyone has, regardless of birthplace or citizenship.

veto: the ability to reject a law or other measure enacted by a legislature.

In order for justice systems and policing to be effective, they must be based on the rule of law. The *rule of law* is a principle whereby the government and its officials, along with all citizens, groups, businesses, and institutions, are subject to rules and regulations that are fair, just, and enforced uniformly. Laws must also be public and widely known. The rule of law is designed to ensure that everyone is treated equally regardless of their social or economic status, or their race, ethnicity, religion, gender, or sexual orientation. Democracies must embrace the rule of law to ensure justice and equality for their citizens.

Violations of the rule of law often occur when officials use their power and authority to treat some individuals or groups differently from others. For instance, authorities might allow one group access to public facilities, but then deny that ability to other groups. In other cases, officials might favor one religion over another when exercising their authority. Even with laws designed to ensure equality and justice, democracies often struggle to maintain the rule of law, especially within the criminal justice system.

The Principles of the Rule of Law

The rule of law is a basic component of democracy and an essential element of fair justice systems. It is based on four main principles. The first, and foremost, principle is that no one is above the law. Everyone, including government officials and workers, as well as the rich and elite, are subject to the same laws. Political power or wealth cannot be used to evade the law or gain advantages in the legal system.

The second principle is that laws protect the basic **human rights** of all citizens. Among the most important rights are those of liberty, security, and property. The justice system should maintain the freedom of its people, as well as protect their lives and safety. It should also protect property, including personal possessions, along with homes, businesses, and farms.

The third principle requires that laws be fair and easily understood. Citizens should be able to have input in the political process whereby new laws are created. That political process should also be transparent. In addition, citizens should know what is legal and what is illegal. This requires governments to publicize new laws and take steps to educate the public about the justice system.

The fourth, and final, principle is that the justice system itself be fair and competent. Fairness in this area requires that the justice system be efficient, free from corruption, and neutral. Efficiency requires adequate resources and competent officials. Those officials should be representative of the communities in which they operate.

U.S. president Lyndon Johnson signs the Civil Rights Act of 1964, which stated that all Americans were to be treated equally, regardless of race. Civil rights leader Dr. Martin Luther King Jr. stands immediately behind Johnson.

RONCARELLI V. DUPLESSIS (1959)

In the 1940s, members of the Jehovah's Witnesses were often subject to discrimination in Canada. They were routinely arrested for distributing religious materials door-to-door, a danger other Christian groups usually did not face. Frank Roncarelli, a Jehovah's Witness in Montreal, Quebec, used profits from his restaurant business to bail out more than 300 members of his religion after they were arrested. This angered Maurice Duplessis, who was the premier (governor) of Quebec. In December 1946, in an attempt to cut Roncarelli's profits of the Jehovah's Witness, Duplessis ordered the government to rescind his liquor license so that his restaurant could not serve alcohol. Roncarelli had to close his business six months later due to falling revenue.

Roncarelli sued Duplessis, and the case eventually reached the Canadian Supreme Court. In 1959, in the case *Roncarelli v. Duplessis*, the Canadian high court ruled that the premier had violated the rule of law by inappropriately using his authority to target Roncarelli because of his religion. The court awarded Roncarelli $33,123.53, plus legal costs. Unfortunately, Roncarelli died before the case was settled (his family received the settlement). The case became an important milestone in ensuring that elected officials in Canada respected the rule of law.

THE RULE OF LAW AND INDIVIDUAL RIGHTS

The rule of law also ensures that people have well-defined rights in the justice system, including **due process**. People suspected of crimes cannot be arrested, detained, or punished without a trial or other appropriate legal action or justification. Nor can property be confiscated by officials without court action. If a police officer witnesses a person committing a crime, the officer can arrest the suspect. However, if police are not present when a crime is committed, they have to gather evidence and then present that information or material to a court official, who will decide if there is enough evidence to justify an arrest. If there is adequate evidence, the official will provide the police with a warrant, or legal document, that authorizes an arrest. Warrants are also generally required to search a person's property, such as their home or work (this is discussed in more detail in the following chapter). This is done to protect not only the person's property, but their privacy as well.

Due process also requires a fair trial. Depending on the legal system and the crime, the evidence at that trial may be assessed by a judge or by a jury of citizens chosen to decide the guilt or innocence of the accused. Many legal systems, especially those based on common law, presume that the accused is innocent, and require the plaintiff to prove the defendant guilty (instead of requiring defendants to prove their innocence). In

The right to a fair trial is a cornerstone of the justice system in a democracy.

HABEAS CORPUS

An important legal right in common law is the ability to file a writ of habeas corpus. Habeas corpus (Latin for "you [shall] have the body") is a request from a prisoner for a court to review his or her detention. It allows people who believe they have been unjustly or wrongfully imprisoned to petition a court to examine the circumstances surrounding their imprisonment. For instance, prisoners can use habeas corpus to challenge a conviction if they believe their original trial violated their rights. Prisoners can also argue that their sentence was too long for the crime.

Australia, Canada, the United States, and other countries, the accused must be proven guilty beyond a reasonable doubt. If convicted of a crime, suspects also typically have the right to **appeal** the verdict to a higher court to ensure that their conviction was proper.

THE RULE OF LAW AND GOVERNMENT POWER

To implement the rule of law, a country must make sure that the law is equally applied to all persons. This has historically proven difficult in some nations. One method adopted by many democracies has been to create a system of **checks and balances** that ensures that the different branches of government play an appropriate role in the justice system. This provides additional oversight of the judicial and criminal justice systems, as well as better protections for the rights of citizens.

Some democratic governments, such as the United States and Germany, divide their political systems into three branches. A nation's legislative branch enacts laws, but those laws are enforced by the executive branch, while the judicial branch oversees both the interpretation of laws and issues surrounding violations of laws and the consequences of those violations. The **chief executive**—often titled president, chancellor, or premier—is elected by the people, and this person then appoints minsters or secretaries to lead the different government agencies.

In other systems, such as Australia and the United Kingdom, there is not a clear separation between the legislative and the executive branches. The chief executive, typically a prime minister, is the leader of the largest party in the legislature. The leaders of the various executive agencies are also chosen from the legislature. Nonetheless, there are still checks and balances on the power of the executive and other branches. For example, in these systems, the prime minister cannot veto legislation as a president can in the U.S. model.

The Federal Administrative Court in Leipzig, Germany.

THE WORLD JUSTICE PROJECT RULE OF LAW INDEX

Each year, the World Justice Project, an international nonprofit organization, conducts surveys of citizens and interviews experts in 102 countries to rate the effectiveness of the rule of law, based on 44 indicators, such as the independence and fairness of the judiciary and the degree of individual freedoms. Listed below are the nations with the strongest and weakest rule of law in 2015, according to this organization. The United States ranked 19th, below France (18th) and above the Czech Republic (20th).

RULE OF LAW, 2015

Countries with the strongest rule of law	Countries with the weakest rule of law
1. Denmark	93. Bangladesh
2. Norway	94. Bolivia
3. Sweden	95. Uganda
4. Finland	96. Nigeria
5. The Netherlands	97. Cameroon
6. New Zealand	98. Pakistan
7. Austria	99. Cambodia
8. Germany	100. Zimbabwe
9. Singapore	101. Afghanistan
10. Australia	102. Venezuela

Source: World Justice Project, "Rule of Law Around the World," 2015. http://worldjusticeproject. org/rule-law-around-world.

The system of checks and balances prevents any one branch of government from dominating the others. For instance, citizens can turn to the judiciary to file grievances against the executive. When members of the executive branch, whether they be elected officials or government workers, such as police officers, exceeds their authority, their actions can be reviewed by the judiciary. Concurrently, if judges or other members of the judiciary misbehave, they can be investigated by the executive branch. The result is a system that can reduce the likelihood of corruption on the part of officials, while ensuring a justice system that is proficient and effective.

TEXT-DEPENDENT QUESTIONS

1. What are the main principles of the rule of law?
2. How does due process protect the rights of individuals in the justice system?
3. What are the major branches of democratic governments, and what functions do they perform?

RESEARCH PROJECTS

1. Research how your local government informs citizens of new laws. Write a report that assesses whether or not the government's efforts are effective in notifying citizens of new laws or changes in existing measures.
2. Choose a country and research its judicial system. Write a brief essay on how that country organizes its judiciary, including the different types of courts and their powers.

CHAPTER FIVE

CHALLENGES

WORDS TO UNDERSTAND

civilian review board: a special body or commission that consists of civilians or nonmembers of a particular police agency who are empowered to investigate corruption and misconduct by law enforcement.

criminal responsibility: the ability of a person to understand the difference between right and wrong, and the consequences of a crime, and thereby be held accountable for her or his actions.

internal affairs: a unit within a law enforcement agency that investigates allegations of misconduct by officials.

police brutality: the use of excessive or disproportionate force by law enforcement officials.

search warrant: a court order that allows law enforcement officials to enter a home, business, or other property to carry out a search for illegal items or evidence related to a crime.

D emocracies face a range of challenges in their efforts to ensure justice, promote fair and effective policing, and maintain the rule of law. One key issue is the need to balance justice for victims against the rights of the accused. In order to prevent people from being convicted for crimes they did not commit, justice systems in democracies offer a variety of protections for the accused, including the presumption of innocence until convicted. These protections may mean that a guilty person goes free in order to prevent innocents from being convicted. Sometimes, for instance, evidence in a crime is gathered illegally. Police may fail to obtain a valid **search warrant** before they seize evidence from a suspect's home or vehicle. When this occurs, often the evidence is not permissible in court.

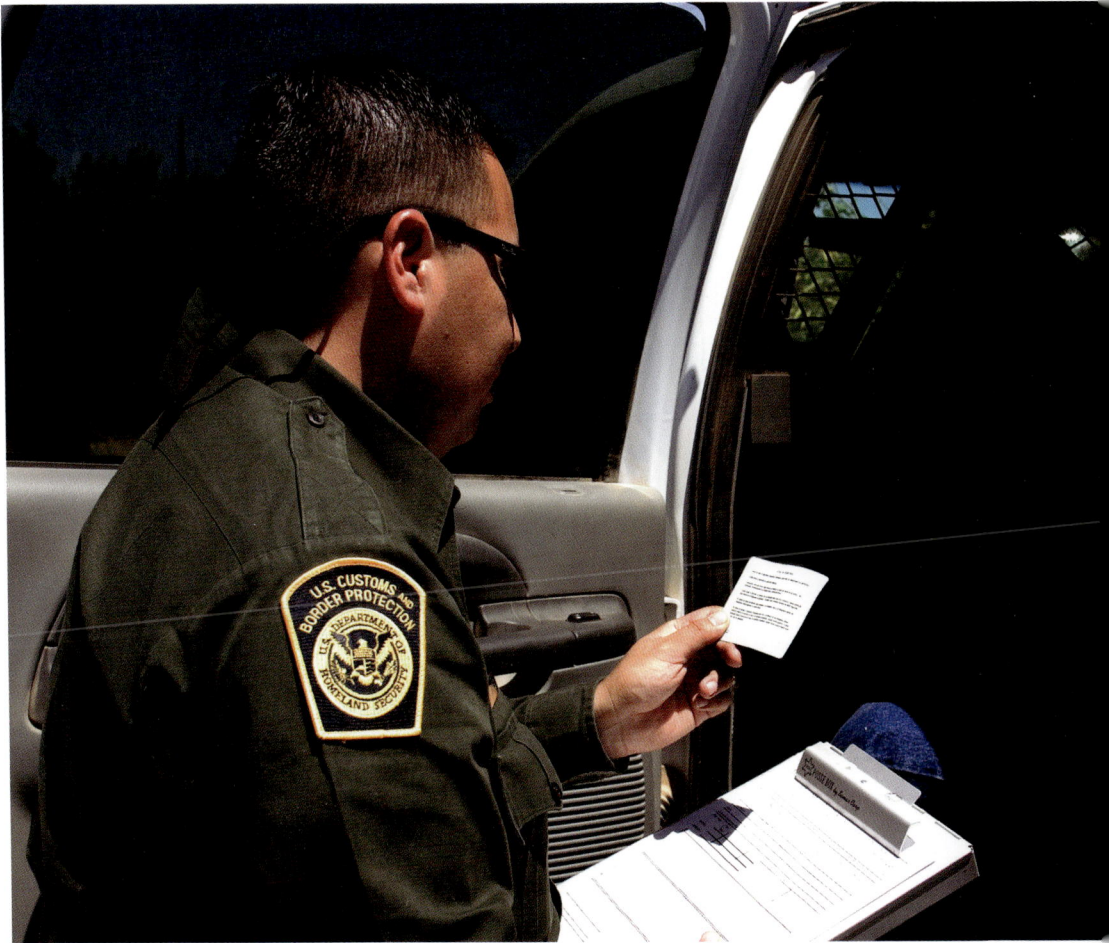

A U.S. Border Patrol agent "mirandizes" a suspect who has just been arrested for transporting drugs over the border.

MIRANDA RIGHTS

In 1963, in Phoenix, Arizona, Ernesto Miranda was arrested for the kidnapping and rape of an 18-year-old. After two hours of interrogations, he confessed to the crime, but at no time did the police inform him that he had the right to an attorney. Miranda was convicted, but he appealed the case. The Supreme Court reviewed the appeal in the case *Miranda v. Arizona*. The Court overturned Miranda's conviction because of the failure of the police to inform him of his rights. Subsequently, all law enforcement officials have had to notify suspects of their rights prior to being arrested or detained. These rights, known "Miranda rights" are usually presented as follows:

> *You have the right to remain silent. Anything you say can and will be used against you in a court of law. You have the right to an attorney. If you cannot afford an attorney, one will be provided for you. Do you understand the rights I have just read to you? With these rights in mind, do you wish to speak to me?*

In Canada, a common version of the warning goes this way:

> *You are under arrest for _____ (insert the charge), do you understand? You have the right to retain and instruct counsel without delay. We will provide you with a toll-free telephone lawyer referral service, if you do not have your own lawyer. Anything you say can be used in court as evidence. Do you understand? Would you like to speak to a lawyer?*

Some justice systems require suspects to have their rights explained to them before they are arrested. In the United States, these are known as a person's Miranda rights, named after a 1966 Supreme Court ruling. In Canada and the United Kingdom, the explanation is known as a caution. These warnings inform suspects that they have the right to an attorney or to remain silent. Not all democracies require suspects to be informed of their rights—Japan does not, for example.

If suspect are not informed of their rights, any evidence gathered through interviewing may be dismissed by a court. The result is that a guilty person may go free because of a mistake made by the justice system. This can undermine the justice system and cause people to lose faith in law enforcement, especially if they believe that criminals are able to evade punishment because of technicalities or legal loopholes.

THE USE OF FORCE

When subduing a suspect, it is sometimes difficult to use just the right amount of force without going too far, especially if the suspect is fighting back. However, some police use excessive force to intimidate suspects or witnesses. This may happen even by mistake. Police brutality is a problem in many law enforcement organizations around the world.

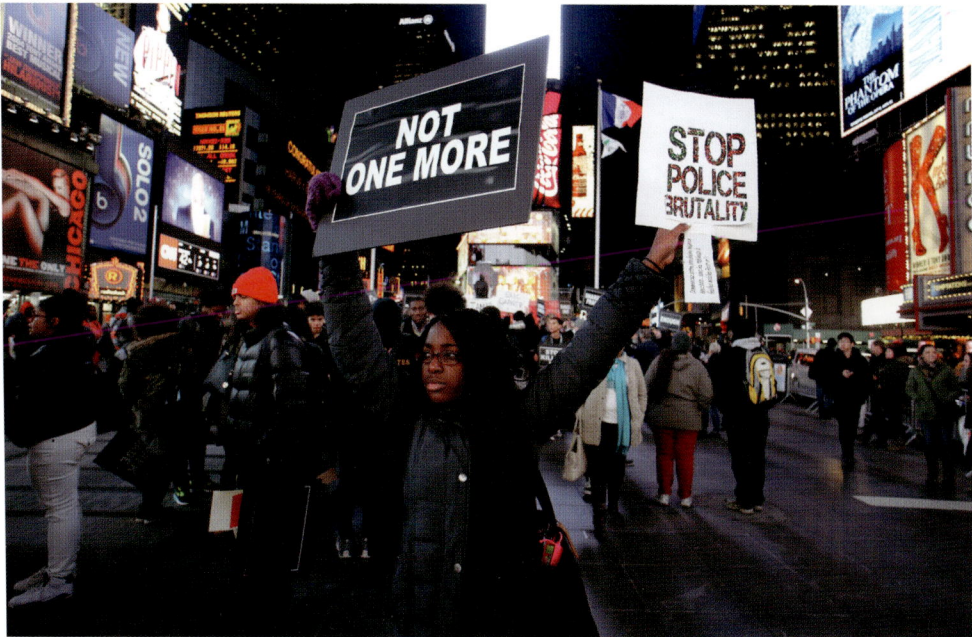

A Black Lives Matter protest in New York City, 2014.

On Green Market Square in Cape Town, South Africa, a banner remembers the 2012 Marikana Massacre. Police opened fire on striking miners, killing 34 and wounding 78.

Like anyone else, law enforcement officials may make mistakes. For example, in 2009 the British police paid out more than $858,000 to cover repairs for properties they had raided inappropriately. Unfortunately, because police have the power to use force, including deadly force, mistakes may have tragic consequences. In Rome, Italy, in 2007, for instance, police fired two shots in the air as a warning in an attempt to stop a fight between two groups of rival soccer fans. One of the bullets struck and killed Gabriele Sandri, a 26-year-old, who was sitting in his car near the incident. The accidental shooting caused widespread rioting and looting.

MINORITY GROUPS AND THE JUSTICE SYSTEM

Even in democracies, minorities and other disadvantaged groups face special challenges in the justice system. In some cases, there may be language or cultural barriers that make it difficult for groups to communicate with law enforcement. New immigrants to a country may not understand the laws or customs of their new home. In other instances, police or justice officials may discriminate against disadvantaged populations because of misperceptions or biases. In some cases, this may make police officers more likely to use force.

This can create a cycle of mistrust and ill will between law enforcement and disadvantaged groups, which can lead to widespread violence. For example, in October 2005, in a suburb of Paris, France, three Muslim youths fled police who were investigating a break-in at a construction site. Two were killed and the third was seriously injured when they were electrocuted trying to hide in a power station. The deaths set off two weeks of riots that killed three people, injured more than 120, and resulted in the arrest of more than 2,800. More than 18,000 police and security officers had to be deployed to stop the unrest. Many of the rioters were recent immigrants from North Africa who were economically disadvantaged and felt isolated from broader French society.

Even when the use of deadly force is ruled to be justified, it can erode public confidence in law enforcement. On August 9, 2014, Michael Brown, an unarmed 18-year-old African American was shot and killed by a police officer in Ferguson, Missouri. The killing prompted a wave of protests, riots, and looting, which intensified after the officer involved was not charged with any wrongdoing. A subsequent investigation into the incident and the Ferguson police force was highly critical of the agency and called for a range of reforms.

The events in Ferguson highlighted issues related to the use of force by U.S. law enforcement. In 2014, more than 1,100 people were killed by police in the United States, while 51 police officers were killed in the line of duty. In comparison, in Iceland, which granted has a tiny population, the police had only killed one person in 71 years (that killing occurred in 2013). In the United States, the protest group Black Lives Matter was created after the Ferguson shooting to focus attention on police shootings of minorities.

Police violence also occurs in other democracies. For instance, in India, concerns have been raised about the excessive use of force against prisoners and detainees. A 2011 report by the Asian Centre for Human Rights asserted that 14,231 people died in police custody between 2001 and 2010. The report accused Indian law enforcement of the excessive use of force and torture in most of the cases.

POLICING THE POLICE

Some law enforcement and justice system officials engage in corruption. This usually occurs in one of two forms. Official corruption involves offenses related to the misconduct. For instance, law enforcement officials might selectively enforce certain laws depending on the race, gender, or ethnicity of the people involved. Or police officers might falsify evidence to help win the conviction of suspects. The second form of corruption involves actions for personal gain, including bribes or theft (including stealing from crime scenes).

To both deter and punish corruption, law enforcement agencies have special units to investigate allegation of corruption. In the United States, this type of unit is usually known as an **internal affairs** division. In the United Kingdom, a national body, the Independent Police Complaints Commission, has the authority to investigate complaints against the police. Many countries, and cities within the United States, also utilize **civilian review boards** to review allegations of corruption or misconduct by law enforcement. These bodies differ from internal affairs units

In Brisbane, Australia, protesters demand justice for Julieka Dhu, who died while in police custody in 2014.

THE CHALLENGES OF JURISDICTIONS

One of the more complicated challenges for both the police and the court system is that of jurisdiction. In many countries, there are multiple law enforcement agencies that have authority over overlapping territory and crimes. In Australia, each state has its own police force with jurisdiction within the state, while there is also a national or federal police force with authority throughout the country. The courts also have overlapping jurisdictions. Countries such as Canada and the United States have similar systems. This overlay of jurisdictions can lead to problems. Different forces may fail to share intelligence with each other, for example. As a result, two agencies might be investigating the same individual for different crimes, and each may have information that could help the other.

A view of the Thousand Island Bridge, which connects New York state with Ontario, Canada.

because they are made up of non-law enforcement officials. The creation of a civilian review board was one of the reforms urged for Ferguson, Missouri, in the wake of the Michael Brown shooting.

CHALLENGES AND RESPONSES FOR LEGAL SYSTEMS

While corruption can be a problem, legal systems in democratic countries also face challenges that are separate and distinct from those that confront the police. For instance, democratic countries around the world have undertaken a variety of reforms to their penal, or prison, systems in an effort to reduce prison populations and make it easier to rehabilitate convicts. As noted above, many countries have embraced restorative justice as an alternative to lengthy prison sentences. In the United States, the federal government has begun a process of reducing prosecutions for nonviolent drug offenses, while also releasing existing prisoners convicted of such offenses.

One of the most significant contemporary challenges has been the high number of youth offenders. In some countries in Europe, such as Belgium or Luxembourg, youths under the age of 18 are not prosecuted for crimes, but are instead dealt with by a juvenile justice system. However, in other democracies, the age of **criminal responsibility** is much younger. It is 10 in England, Northern Ireland, and Wales, and even younger in some states in the United States. In Nevada and Washington it is 8, and in Oklahoma it is 7, while the majority of U.S. states do not have a minimum age. One result is that the United States is the only country in the world with youth offenders (people under the age of 18) serving life sentences without parole. There were more than 2,500 youths serving such sentences in adult prisons in the United States in 2012.

Reforms and efforts to prevent corruption are critically important for justice systems. In order for the system to work, people must trust and respect law enforcement and the courts. These systems rely on the cooperation of citizens during investigations and in efforts to deter and reduce crime. When people feel that the police or the courts do not have their best interests at heart, they become alienated and uncooperative. The resulting tension is manifested in incidents such as what happened in Ferguson, Missouri. On the other hand, a professional, fair, and efficient justice system is the best way to ensure the rule of law and maintain justice and equality.

TEXT-DEPENDENT QUESTIONS

1. What is the most difficult challenge facing democracies in their justice systems?
2. What impact does police brutality have on communities?
3. What steps can be undertaken to deter and punish corruption within law enforcement?

RESEARCH PROJECTS

1. Research the use of force by police. Create a chart that lists the steps that communities can undertake to reduce violence by law enforcement, without an increase in crime.
2. Research what the age of criminal responsibility is in your country or state. Write a report that examines whether that age is appropriate for someone to be held responsible for their actions.

FURTHER READING

BOOKS

Dammer, Harry R., and Jay S. Albanese. *Comparative Criminal Justice Systems.* 5th ed. Belmont, CA: Wadsworth, 2014.

Ebbe, Obi N. Ignatius, ed. *Comparative and International Justice Systems: Policing, Judiciary, and Corrections.* Oxford: Butterworth-Heinemann, 2000.

Perez, Douglas W., and J. Alan Moore. *Police Ethics: A Matter of Character.* 2nd ed. Clifton Park, NY: Delmar Cengage, 2013.

Sandel, Michael J., ed. *Justice: A Reader.* Oxford: Oxford University Press, 2007.

Terrill, Richard J. *World Criminal Justice Systems: A Comparative Survey.* 8th ed. Waltham, MA: Anderson Publishing, 2013.

ONLINE

European Forum for Restorative Justice. http://www.euforumrj.org/.

International Institute for Restorative Practices. http://www.realjustice.org/.

Knafo, Saki. "How Aggressive Policing Affects Police Officers Themselves." *The Atlantic,* July 13, 2015. http://www.theatlantic.com/business/archive/2015/07/aggressive-policing-quotas/398165/.

SERIES GLOSSARY

accountability: making elected officials and government workers answerable to the public for their actions, and holding them responsible for mistakes or crimes.

amnesty: a formal reprieve or pardon for people accused or convicted of committing crimes.

anarchist: a person who believes that government should be abolished because it enslaves or otherwise represses people.

assimilation: the process through which immigrants adopt the cultural, political, and social beliefs of a new nation.

autocracy: a system of government in which a small circle of elites holds most, if not all, political power.

belief: an acceptance of a statement or idea concerning a religion or faith.

citizenship: formal recognition that an individual is a member of a political community.

civil law: statutes and rules that govern private rights and responsibilities and regulate noncriminal disputes over issues such as property or contracts.

civil rights: government-protected liberties afforded to all people in democratic countries.

civil servants: people who work for the government, not including elected officials or members of the military.

corruption: illegal or unethical behavior on the part of officials who abuse their position.

democracy: A government in which the people hold all or most political power and express their preferences on issues through regular voting and elections.

deportation: the legal process whereby undocumented immigrants or those who have violated residency laws are forced to leave their new country.

dual citizenship: being a full citizen of two or more countries.

election: the process of selecting people to serve in public office through voting.

expatriate: someone who resides in a country other than his or her nation of birth.

feminism: the belief in social, economic, and political equality for women.

gender rights: providing access to equal rights for all members of a society regardless of their gender.

glass ceiling: obstacles that prevent the advancement of disadvantaged groups from obtaining senior positions of authority in business, government, and education.

globalization: a trend toward increased interconnectedness between nations and cultures across the world; globalization impacts the spheres of politics, economics, culture, and mass media.

guest workers: citizens of one country who have been granted permission to temporarily work in another nation.

homogenous: a region or nation where most people have the same ethnicity, language, religion, customs, and traditions.

human rights: rights that everyone has, regardless of birthplace or citizenship.

incumbent: an official who currently holds office.

industrialization: the transformation of social life resulting from the technological and economic developments involving factories.

jurisdiction: the official authority to administer justice through activities such as investigations, arrests, and obtaining testimony.

minority: a group that is different—ethnically, racially, culturally, or in terms of religion— within a larger society.

national security: the combined efforts of a country to protect its citizens and interests from harm.

naturalization: the legal process by which a resident noncitizen becomes a citizen of a country.

nongovernmental organization (NGO): a private, nonprofit group that provides services or attempts to influence governments and international organizations.

oligarchy: a country in which political power is held by a small, powerful, but unelected group of leaders.

partisanship: a strong bias or prejudice toward one set of beliefs that often results in an unwillingness to compromise or accept alternative points of view.

refugees: people who are kicked out of their country or forced to flee to another country because they are not welcome or fear for their lives.

right-to-work laws: laws in the United States that forbid making union membership a condition for employment.

secular state: governments that are not officially influenced by religion in making decisions.

sexism: system of beliefs, or ideology, that asserts the inferiority of one sex and justifies discrimination based on gender.

socialist: describes a political system in which major businesses or industries are owned or regulated by the community instead of by individuals or privately owned companies.

socioeconomic status: the position of a person within society, based on the combination of their income, wealth, education, family background, and social standing.

sovereignty: supreme authority over people and geographic space. National governments have sovereignty over their citizens and territory.

theocracy: a system of government in which all major decisions are made under the guidance of religious leaders' interpretation of divine authority.

treason: the betrayal of one's country.

tyranny: rule by a small group or single person.

veto: the ability to reject a law or other measure enacted by a legislature.

wage gap: the disparity in earnings between men and women for their work.

INDEX

ABOUT THE AUTHOR

Tom Lansford is a Professor of Political Science, and a former academic dean, at the University of Southern Mississippi, Gulf Coast. He is a member of the governing board of the National Social Science Association and a state liaison for Mississippi for Project Vote Smart. His research interests include foreign and security policy, and the U.S. presidency. Dr. Lansford is the author, coauthor, editor or coeditor of more than 40 books, and the author of more than one hundred essays, book chapters, encyclopedic entries, and reviews. Recent sole-authored books include: *A Bitter Harvest: U.S. Foreign Policy and Afghanistan* (2003), the *Historical Dictionary of U.S. Diplomacy Since the Cold War* (2007) and *9/11 and the Wars in Afghanistan and Iraq: A Chronology and Reference Guide* (2011). His more recent edited collections include: *America's War on Terror* (2003; second edition 2009), *Judging Bush* (2009), and *The Obama Presidency: A Preliminary Assessment* (2012). Dr. Lansford has served as the editor of the annual *Political Handbook of the World* since 2012.

PHOTO CREDITS